Philosophies of Wisdom
to Sanity
James Peebles Jr
San Diego,Ca.

These are words to live by as I've experienced life. Some of these truths were learned by me with much pain although saved my life many times. I've learned these lessons with a thankful heart and a painful soul.

These truths work. And I've found them most helpful in times of trouble. May you learn what I took a lifetime from colleges and institutions. Most of everything I've written is taken from thousands of books and many Phd's. This is a luxury for you to have in one book what took me a lifetime of learning in a condensed written form. I hope you enjoy reading this book and find it amusing and helpful while teaching you the lessons of life.

Who can honestly tell you what you are? Only God can. Others opinions aren't always facts.

You are, as you think.

No one has to give you permission to be yourself. Only you can.

Life isn't always fair until the last inning. Then a home run can be hit and change the whole ball game.

No one can make you who you are. God can. You can just help by doing your best, and following him the best that you're able.

I'm a human being, not a human doing it.

You don't have to be validated for the truth that you already know.

You can't be a friend unless you both agree you are. You can't make it happen. It has to be given with free will.

You can't make anything happen. If it doesn't.

You can't make someone change to be who they're not. If you try, it's not them who's changed. It's you.

Thinking bad thoughts can't be good. Thinking good thoughts can't be bad.

You can't steal what you already own.

One with few friends. Can be more of a friend.

I can learn more from people I don't like. Than people I do.

It's not the politicians who make the laws. It's the people who really elect them that do.

Republicans, Democrates, and Independents. Are like vinegar, spices, and oil. They all make the salad.

You can't make the truth out of nothing if it didn't happen.

Time doesn' change. I do.

You can't satisfy an appetite. Without hunger.

A little of something is better. Than a lot of nothing.

Just because it's right. Doesn't make it so.

If you knew everything. There'd be nothing to know.

You never had what you can't lose.

Which would you rather be? Famous and dead or alive and unknown?

If time is money. Then prisons are full of billionaires.

Everyone dies but not everyone lives.

Anger is like drinking poison and expecting the other to die instead of yourself.

If money is the root of all evil. Then what's the flower?

Don't piss on big dogs. Cats are debatable.

Love takes no prisoners that are free.

Music is sound through the ear to the soul.

Some ideas are like diamonds in the coal mine of your head.

You can judge a man by the words they use. Mostly by the ones they don't but want to.

If the world's a stage. And we're all actors. Then get me some popcorn and a Coke during intermission.

If you have nothing. You have nothing to lose. If you do. You have everything to lose.

Who's richer? The one who has wealth or the one who will become rich with their life?

If love is free. I need a discount.

Who's wiser? The one who knows or the one that wants to be wise?

No pain, no gain. Then hospitals are full of winners.

What doesn't kill you only makes you stronger. Unless you're dead.

You can't prove love. It proves itself. It doesn't need help. If you do. Then it isn't love.

Reality doesn't have to make sense. Fiction does.

The less you know. The more you can learn.

A great artist creates nothing. That isn't there.

A thought is like a seed. Planted in the mind.

You never have enough money to spend on what you don't have. You have enough for what you do.

I'd rather feel I'm in Love. Than think it.

One who has everything. Has nothing.

One who is nobody to others is somebody to themselves.

You can't teach someone what they already know. If you do. You're only teaching yourself what you know. Not them.

My mind has a mind of it's own.

To find a diamond takes no talent. To cut it takes skill.

One who knows everything. Has nothing to learn.

You can't Love. What isn't there.

You don't choose Love. It chooses it's own.

Hate is like digging three graves. Your's and the other's and God's.

You can't Love and Hate at the same time. If you do. You'll only kill one.

You can't make up the truth.

Life and Death are the same. Only from a different perspective.

You can't learn a lesson. Without a problem. And that's the solution.

You can't decide. What you don't know.

If all is one. Then you're really alone. It takes two to tango.

If I wasn't created. Why am I here?

If life is an illusion. Then please tell Citibank.

If there is no such thing as cause and effect. Then what caused this effect that I am?

If evolution is real and we came from apes. Why haven't the other apes in the zoo become human? I guess that's natural selection. Don't tell the other apes because you might make them angry.

Maybe I was wrong and Lucy was one of the first evolving humans. I can testify to this. I know some people that have the same features.

There is no right or wrong. It just is. Tell that to the next Police Officer when he stops you for speeding.

If life is a joke. What's the punch line?

The fastest speed is arriving. Before you even start.

A performer needs an audience. With out one they can't perform. An audience is as important as the artist.

There's no such thing as bad art. As there's no such thing as a wrong thought. All art is an expression of thoughts.

Living is an art. In the studio called Earth.

Creativity is nothing without imagination.

If you made everyone think like you do. You'd know nothing.

You can't believe what you don't know.

You can't teach a man what they don't want.

The problem in questioning authority. Is asking the right questions.

My favorite sound is silence.

A scholar writes what they've learned. An artist writes what they dream.

Every rose has thorns. As everyone has a past.

You can't drive someone crazy. They have to do their own driving.

You can't forget Love. It forgets you.

You can't be full. Unless you're first empty.

If you're chasing a carrot. Cut the string.

You can't get to Heaven in your head.

Knowledge can't be taught. It has to be learned.

A gem is as rare as a human is. All unique with different values.

If life is a test. Get Cliff's notes.

The less you have. The more value it has.

We are all threads. In the tapestry called life.

Asking the wrong person. Can't give you the right answer.

The truth is absolute. There can't be more.

Time has no limit forever.

You can't pretend what is real.

Once a word is spoken. It can't go back into your mouth.

You can't talk about someone behind their back. In front of them.

You can't be sorry. For what you haven't done.

You can't settle an argument by yourself.

You don't win a war. Without peace.

You don't have to defend yourself. If no one is attacting you.

It takes two people for an argument. Any less. Is insanity.

Peace does't hide. People do.

Emotions speak louder than words.

Unsettled disagreements. Is like leaving a campfire smoldering unattended.

If the shoe fits. Don't take it back.

You can't understand. What you don't know.

You can't wear out. New ideas.

The smartest person in the world and the fool were born alike.

A wise person is as wise. As a fool is foolish.

Everything can't be seen. With the eyes.

You don't have to justify. The truth.

A large bank account. Is never big enough. For the thrifty.

One can't change their life. To what. It isn't.

You can't talk yourself. Out of the truth.

If the truth isn't so important. Why do we need it?

If lies are here today. Gone tomorrow. What about next week?

If you can't change a horse in midstream. How about the other side?

You can't spend invisible money. Unless you got a credit card.

You can't plan. For the inevitable.

You can't be. A sinner and a Saint. At the same time.

If we let go. What do we hold on to?

You can't wait for eternity.

You can't learn what you don't want to.

Once something is gone. You'll know what you had.

What ever is meant to be. Will be.

You can only do what you're able.

You can't see what isn't there. Until it's gone.

You can't write about nothing. If you do. That will be something.

The mind incubates ideas. As the farmer incubates eggs.

You can't be right and wrong. At the same time.

Pleasure is never satisfied. Until it's over.

Not knowing. Is also a form. Of knowing.

Not getting an answer. Is also getting an answer.

You can't give. What isn't yours.

Speaking and living a truth. Are two different things.

In court you'll never get justice. Just a verdict.

You can't control life. Only manage it.

All life makes sense. If you've got the correct information.

You'll never catch a fish. Until you go fishing.

Finding your purpose in life is only half the battle. The other half. Is living it out.

You can only Love a person once. If you rekindle that Love. It's the same Love.

There's only one way to quit an addiction. Fill in the whole. With more Love of something else.

If the mind is starved. There's little energy for the body.

Curiosity is the fuel that feeds the brain to live.

I rather live and be happy in my mind. Than take pleasure in my body. At the expense of my spirit.

You can never learn too much. There's too much to know. And so little time to try.

You can't make peace with existence. If you're at war with yourself.

If someone doesn't like you. Be thankful they're not your friend.

You can't live a lie. And be true to yourself.

I'd rather know little. Than know too much.

I'd rather own just enough. Than have everything I want.

The only difference between. Being happy and sad. Is perspective.

You can't question reality. As it is. You can. Only it won't do any good.

Sometimes you have too much. Of what you don't want. Yet sometimes you have enough. Of what you do.

You can't tell someone the truth. If they don't want to hear it.

You'll know you've arrived. When you're there.

To know a lot. Is that you know. You know little.

Gratitude and anger. Can't live in the same room.

There can't be winners. Without losers.

If more people die of obesity in the world. Why do millions starve?

Nothing is sacred. That isn't believed in.

One can't have faith and doubt. At the same time.

You can't Love. What you don't know.

There's always more. Of what you don't have. And less of. What you want.

You can't trade happiness for fear. Or generousity. For greed.

I wouldn't need to judge. If I had no opinion.

If you don't like who you are. You're in bad company.

You can't spend time. Without saving a little.

You can't hit a home run. Unless you swing for one.

No one can hurt you. Unless you care.

One can't make a lie. Out of the truth. Anymore than dishonor. Out of honor. In the end.

You can't tell a pig to fly. You'll only make it mad.

Respect can be best a plural word not singular. Actions speak louder than words.

To live a lie. Is to die.

Out of the five stages of grief or death. The two most important ones are left out. Forgiving and forgetting.

One with nothing. Has everything to gain.

If life didn't matter. There'd be no God.

You can't create friends. They make themselves.

Friendships can't be planned. Anymore than a beautiful sunset.

Being alone is an art. Being with others is a skill.

Reality and fantasy don't have to make sense, yet money can.

To honor others. Is to honor yourself.

One can't live a lie. Dead.

You can't buy value out of worthlessness.

If money makes you happy. What's the cost?

The best weapons in war. Are love and forgiveness.

You can't take time. Without first making it.

You can't live well with others. If you can't with yourself.

You can't hurt anyone. If they don't care.

You can't learn the truth. If you don't use it.

You can't love others. Without first loving yourself.

The best way to beat anger. Is to be indifferent.

No one can hurt you. If you don't judge.

You can't feel pleasure. Without pain.

You can't do anything. Unless you're able.

You can't learn a lesson. Without a problem.

You can't give to others. What you don't have yourself.

We can project on to others. What we don't see of ourselves.

If you test someone for something. You don't trust them. Otherwise you'd just ask.

Trust is a two way street in the highway of life.

There can't be intimacy. Without trust.

Forgiveness is a meal. Best served warm.

Perspectives have many truths. Absolutes don't. There is only one truth.

You can't make a blind man see. As you can't make a deaf man hear. And an angry man can't have peace.

You can't trust someone. Who can't trust themselves.

If you can't trust yourself. You can't trust others.

One can't hate people. And love peace.

If you can't forgive yourself. You can't forgive others.

Question reality. And reality will question you.

Love doesn't question. It only answers.

Hate is like poison. It can kill you.

Hate is a feeling. Not just a word.

If you want to have pleasant feelings. Think pleasant thoughts.

Someday the truth will finally be. Until then we must use patience.

You can't make an angry person happy. By agreeing with them.

You can't forgive. Unless you care.

You can't spoil someone. That loves others as much as they love themselves.

The best revenge is peace that takes time.

One can't have problems. And not expect answers.

There are usually two or more sides to every story. Depending on who's side you're on. The truth is absolute.

If there are many paths to the same summit. How many are dead ends?

It takes no bravery to judge someone behind their back. It takes courage to judge someone to their face.

Who ever gossips to you. Usually gossips about you.

If you give your word. You ought to keep it.

Honesty can't be bought. Dishonesty can.

We forget what we don't practice.

The most complicated question. Is best said with the simplest answer.

To forgive someone is the beginning of understanding them.

A liar. Can't believe the truth.

You can't save life's. By killing.

You can't kill. With the truth.

Love is equal to all. No one can love you more.

You love yourself by loving others. You love others by loving yourself.

If you want to know someone. Ask who they love. Then ask why.

You don't lose. What you can't have.

I can't find solutions. Without problems.

If you want to be kind. First love yourself. Then others.

Sometimes problems can teach. Sometimes pain can too.

If you don't know the truth. You know nothing.

There are many paths in life. Our job is to avoid the dead ends.

Honest people don't deceive others. Dishonest people choose so.

If you're in the business of hurting others. You should go bankrupt.

You can't expect justice. From people who don't practice it.

You can't expect maturity. From people who don't understand what it means.

You can't teach a fool wisdom. If they don't want to learn it.

Cruelty can be taught. It has to be chosen to be learned.

Keeping away from fools. Is to be wise.

You can't sell the essence of truth. It's free and can't be sold.

You can't be at peace. With immaturity. If you are. Then you're not.

You can't hurt people. If they don't have a heart.

If life doesn't make sense. You've lost your feelings.

Who can tell you a lie? If you don't listen.

You can't change Love. Love changes you.

A fool. Knows nothing about peace.

The one who has less to say. Usually makes their point better.

You can say more. With little.

Your body speaks more. Than your mouth.

Love changes no one. Except it's own.

Gossipers try to assassinate others character. Not knowing in the end they did theirs.

It's hard to be fair. With someone who isn't just.

It's hard to learn life's lessons. Unless you're tested.

You can't talk back to someone who's not there. And have them listen.

You can hurt someone much worse with words. Than actions. The spirit is more sensitive than the whole body.

You can Love your enemies. By giving them time and space.

One who says hurtful things about someone behind their back. Usually is a coward and can't say it to their face.

You Love someone more. By telling your truth.

If you expect nothing. You won't regret anything.

You can't expect someone to like you. If they don't.

You can't play fair. With cheaters.

It takes courage to stand up for yourself. Alone in adversity.

One can be fair and confident. With the trustworthy.

You can wound or heal with your speech.

If you really want things to end. Don't start something.

You can't have a war. If you don't fight.

You have a better chance of winning in life. If you don't keep everybody's score.

If you want to get along with your enemies. Keep away from them.

What fools and enemies have in common is. They both don't need your company.

An enemy is easy to spot. They want to do you harm.

If you can live better with others than yourself. You've lost yourself.

You have peace through sanity.

Love is more of a verb. Than a noun. I wish people were like this.

Philosophies aren't the same. For good reason.

You can't control others. At best. Only manage yourself.

You can't hurt someone. Without effecting others.

Ignorance costs more. Than reality.

You can't stop someone that already did something. Once they've already done it.

You can't make someone like you. That's their job.

You can't have peace through war.

If someone has certain problems you don't. Thank God you're not them.

Why expect justice, integrity, ethics, wisdom, accountability, and morals from fools? Unless you are one.

You can't expect good people to forgive the crimes of others. Unless they committed one themselves.

A fool can never understand truth, logic, or reality.

People who say they're a genius. Are like a prisoner bragging about how large their prison cell is.

Perfectionist have the dream of control. Anarchists have the dream of chaos. Realist need neither.

If everything were written. Literature would have ended.

Homelessness isn't a place. It's a state of mind.

Ignorance can't be taught. It has to be learned.

It takes no instruction to be a fool.

I rather be poor and alone. Than rich and lose my privacy and peace.

The difference between war and peace. Are actions.

You can't reason with a fool. Unless you are one.

If someone wants to hurt you. They can't if you're gone. Not just outside. Inside. Detach.

How do you detach? With others? Go inside of your mind and find something else good.

How do you find good if it's not there? Pretend it's a dream. Then live it.

There's only three ways someone can hurt you. Physically and Mentally and Spiritually.

You can't be hurt if no one has a chance. Stay away from fools inside your mind and outside your body if you can. If not do nothing. If you can't do anything else. You've lost.

All wars have a time limit. So does peace. Abusers aren't in charge. If you are.

All conflicts are lost and won in the mind. It takes a strong mind to resolve differences.

What's the best way to detach? Surrender control.

You can't believe. What you don't understand.

You can't win a game. If you don't know the rules. It's the same with life.

You'll never hurt someone you know. That doesn't have feelings about you.

One can't win a war with a fool. Fools don't understand what peace is.

The toughest war. You'll ever face. Is with yourself.

You'll never lose a war. You never fought.

The best revenge. Is a healthy attitude.

You never lost an argument. You didn't have.

You never win a fight. Unless it ends.

Freedom is a state of mind. Not a location.

You can't be free. Until you think you are.

No one can lock you up. If you have the key.

Your job isn't to find the key to life. Your job is to find the lock of it. Then the key. Then unlock it.

You can't victimize. A hero.

Your enemy will never give you peace. You already have.

Revenge costs more. Than forgiveness.

You can't give Love. If you don't Love yourself. You can't give what you don't have.

If you give with no strings attached. That's a gift. Otherwise it's a business transaction.

One can't live rent free. In a healthy mind.

You can never get away from yourself or others. You live with them forever somewhere in your mind.

Two of the most important traits I value in a person. Are kindness and honestly.

You can forgive anybody. If you can forgive yourself.

One can't live in the past. To change the present. Only by living in the present. Can we create the future.

Nothing can bother you. That you don't think about.

If you want to forget your problems. Don't remember them.

Peace starts from inside your mind. Not outside.

Nothing can upset you. If you don't believe it does.

You can be happy. If you think so.

No one can steal your spirt. If you don't sell your soul.

You're never alone. If you treat yourself as a guest.

If you need forgiveness. And don't forgive others. You're a guilty hypocrite.

Justice isn't only between right and wrong. It's more about evil and righteousness.

You can't judge the innocent to be guilty. And expect justice for yourself.

We were created to be who we are. Not who we're not. Our problem is to find out which.

If someone wants to pick a bone with you. Tell them to look in their closet.

If you can't forget your enemies. Remember your friends.

You'll never appreciate sweet fragrance more. Until you experience foul stench.

You can't make the deft hear. What the blind see. And a liar find the truth.

You can't Love. What you don't feel. And live in reality.

Most problems we have with others. Isn't others. It's our memory of them.

One can't make others feel. What they do. If they're paralyzed.

You can't see the truth. If you live in the dark.

You can never get enough information. If you don't know where to get it.

You'll never get the right answer. If you don't ask the correct question.

The truth doesn't always. Have to make sense.

You can't change the absolute truth. Unless you're a liar.

You can't improve perfection. If you do you're flawed.

You can't condemn someone of something. That you've done yourself. And be fair.

The written interpreted law means nothing. Without the spirit of truth.

You don't respect the law. If you don't keep it.

One ought to believe the truth. Even if it's not told.

Gossip doesn't build bridges. It puts up walls.

It might be the straw on the camel's back that caused something. Only it's more of the camel that did it.

What's fair. Is prosperity for all. What's unfair. Is greed for the few.

Ideas don't just come out of thin air. They're created.

You can't deal in the currency of logic. If you don't make sense.

Some argue we live in a Republic. Some say Democracy. I say we live in freedom. What ever that label is.

There are really only five forces that control our economy. Addition, subtraction, multiplication, division, and people.

We forget. Philosophies may sound logical. Only they're just basically opinions.

You can't have an opinion. Unless you judge.

I'd rather have peace. Than be right.

It's hard to forget. What you don't want to remember

What sounds too good to be true. Usually is.

If you pay all your dues. You got credit for. You debt is paid.

You can't give credit. To those who haven't earned it.

You can never earn grace by what you do. Or don't do. It's a gift. Given free.

Financial records don't always prove good credit. The person who pays for it does.

A gratuity is voluntary. Not mandatory. Otherwise it's not earned as intended.

Faith is the substance of things hoped for. The evidence of things unseen.

One doesn't subtract Love by giving it away. One multiplies it.

Don't talk to people. Who won't listen.

If in life you're the star and producer of your own movie. You're in the audience too.

True art is the interpretation of something. Not the originator. Art just happens as is.

It's hard to live a sane life for yourself. Because others might want a crazy world of their own.

Fools think addictions will end. Over and over again. Reasoning problems will be solved.

Smokers can't see their lungs or smell their smell. Yet hurt themselves and others much.

Treat others like you'd like to be treated yourself. Then hopefully. They will too.

You can't sell pyromaniacs. Fire extinguishers. And you can't sell the guilty. Innocence.

A lie detector might tell if someone lies. What it can do is speculate the truth. Not tell facts.

If a sociopath is after you. Get away. Sociopaths are dangerous and have no conscience.

Some say justice is blind. Tell that to a high priced lawyer.

Oppression is a fact. The oppressors usually deny.

You can't get justice. From dishonesty.

Your life can't be like a song. If you don't know the lyrics and melody.

You can't see accurately what you've done. From somebody's else's eyes.

You can't defend yourself. If nobody's there.

Telling your truth. Does no good. If no one believes you.

One can't pretend. Reality. Realitiy is the truth. It needs no explanation.

You'll never know what life has meant. Until it's over.

Two of the best ways to stay safe. Is to protect your mind and heart.

You can't judge right or wrong. If you don't have the right frame of reference.

You can't make trouble. If you don't get into it.

If you're acting. You're auditioning for a part.

One of my most favorite teachers in life. Is my conscience.

If you want your life to smell like a rose. Don't be foul.

Cheaters can't win. If you don't play with them.

If three or more people say the same thing to you. There's usually a grain of truth to it.

If you think someone is abusing you. Chances are they are.

If someone abused you once. They usually don't stop on their own.

Cruelty by someone. Is justice to another.

One of the best of revenges. Is the conscience. Unless there is none.

If you're in a relationship with someone you don't like. Stop dancing with them.

Injustice says more about the perpetrators. Than the victims.

The passive aggressive usually don't play by the rules. So don't play their game.

An abuser covers up their tracks. Others can't see. And you usually can't prove it.

Don't ever say, "I'll get you for that!" Wait for God; he'll settle the score. 20:22 Proverbs MSG

...for all have sinned and fall short of the glory of God. 3:23 Romans NKJV

...did not do it to one of the least of these, you did not do it to me. 25:45 Matthew NKJV

Let angry people endure the backlash of their own anger; if you try to make it better, you'll only make it worse. 19:19 Proverbs MSG

The more quiet you are. The louder noise becomes.

You can be more thankful for the things you don't have. Than the things you do.

If you really know who you are. It doesn't matter what others do.

Just because there's a garage. Doesn't mean there's a car in it.

It's not fear of fear that's the problem. It's doubt.

You can't live your life. In somebody's else's shoes.

You can't remember. What you never knew.

If you can't learn a lesson. You never had a problem.

Just because something's fancy doesn't make it better. Simplicity is better than complexity.

People who don't experience love. Punish those who do.

Frustration's a cover. For anger.

Just because something costs a lot. Doesn't make it valuable.

Injustice is normal. To the abnormal.

You can't trust people. That aren't accountable.

One can't be smart. Without learning how.

Everyone is important. To themselves.

If I could have anything. I'd want to want nothing.

If I could know everything. I'd want not to know.

You can't win a game . If you don't know the difference.

Real wealth. Can't be measured.

No one is intelligent. That doesn't think first.

You can't tell a fool. Good advice to learn.

You'll never really know what it's like to win.
Until you lose.

You can't live someone else's life. That's their job.

Computers don't have curiosity. They can't love either.

If someone seems perfect. They haven't learned their lessons by making mistakes.

Mistakes aren't problems. Without lessons.

You can't lose anything. You don't have.

You can't love. What you don't like.

Gratitude is depression's worst enemy.

You can't be a friend to anyone. Without first being a friend to yourself.

Insanity has no logic. If it did. That's insane.

Everything can be taken away from you. Except your perspective.

If you can't play by the rules. You're not a participant.

Logic and nonsense. Never get along.

Humility has a front seat. In the banquet of honor.

Usually one can't hurt anyone. Without first being hurt.

A gift is free. A present has social strings attached.

If you can't get along with yourself. Chances are you can't get along with others.

Common sense. Makes no sense to an idiot.

If you want to know if someone loves you. First ask yourself if you love them. Then ask why and how you feel with them. The rest is fate.

You can't hurt someone who has no feelings. It's the same for love.

One can't be in love with a fool. And be wise.

My mind's too active. A million theories are too many. A single philosophy is not enough.

Sometimes failure. Is the best lesson learned.

Intelligence can't be taught. It has to be learned.

You can't stop adversity. Yet you can build tolerance.

One can't learn the lesson. If they don't take the test.

You can't fail in life. And not learn a lesson.

One can do more with an open hand. Than a fist.

If you don't learn a lesson. You've never been taught.

Crazy people usually don't learn. What a wise man teaches.

You only learn. What you need to know.

There's a little insanity in the wise. As there's a little wisdom in a fool.

To really know. Is to know when you don't.

You learn more through adversity. Than through prosperity.

One is really lucky. When one doesn't need it.

Pain is a lesson. That ends with pleasure.

Ignorance leaves. When knowledge enters.

Stench is fragrance to a fool.

Understanding and ignorance are both mortal enemies.

One who plants seeds of hate. Harvests a crop of chaos and destruction.

One can't know God. Without knowing the difference between good and evil.

What accountability and responsibility have in common. Is the truth.

If you don't know the answer. Ask a question.

Disabilities are the gifts of adversity.

Time stands still. When you're bored.

You can't get rich. Without first being poor.

You can't feel pleasure. Without first feeling pain.

If I couldn't judge. I'd have no opinion. If I had no opinion. I couldn't debate. If I couldn't debate it would be one sided. I'd have no freedom to disagree. I'd be a slave.

All friendships are a reflection of yourself.

How you judge others. Is how you will be judged.

Fools remember. What the wise forget.

You can't act your way out of feeling. Yet you can think your way out of acting.

When you tell someone to shut up. You're really saying I don't respect you.

You can be heard more with a quiet voice. Than a loud one.

If you don't like who you are. Change your thoughts.

The best way to deal with a problem. Is to fix it if you can. Then remember it no longer if you can't.

You can't be more of. Who you're not.

Sometimes fools. Can be the greatest teachers.

Something is only learned. If it makes sense to you.

If you sleep with your foes. You'll aweak with your enemies.

One can't believe. If they don't have faith.

If you know you can't win. Don't participate.

You can't lose a fight. If you don't.

You've never lost a war. You never fought.

Forgiveness is more powerful. Than revenge.

It takes more bravery not to fight at the right time. Than to.

Peace is a state of mind. Not circumstances.

One can learn a lot. By being still.

You can't live with God. By yourself.

If all my wishes came true. I'd want nothing.

The less you know. The less you want. The more you have.

Silence is useless. Without noise.

One can't hit a home run. On a golf course.

The wise can thank a fool for his lessons.

Right and wrong are in our perspectives.

There may be many paths to the same summit. Only there's only one trail to the top.

Your body can be a reflection of your mind.

You can't talk your way into Heaven. You have to live your way in.

No one can live up to your standards. If you're looking down on them.

If you're angry at someone. You're really angry with yourself.

You can't hurt someone. Without hurting yourself.

You can't love a loser. And not win.

You can't beat someone at chess. If you're playing checkers.

A fool. Doesn't need to take lessons.

Time never passes. To learn something new.

You can't hurt yourself. And not hurt others.

Try as you may. You can't stop a jerk from being a jerk. It isn't going to happen.

Pain and discomfort. Can teach us many lessons.

To know. And not do. Is to not know.

You can't love evil. Without first hating good.

You're not accountable. For what you can't do.

Feelings are neutral. Reacting to them is what makes them meaningful.

You can't control fate. The best you can do is manage it.

You can't make peace with anyone. Without first making peace with yourself.

You're never alone. If you love yourself.

Fear is. Anxiety turned inward.

You can't change someone's perspective. Without their permission.

You can give your life away. And still keep it.

One can't make a fool be ignorant. That's their job.

You can't hate someone for being stupid. And be smart.

Hurt people. Hurt others.

It's harder to ask the right question. Than get the wrong answer.

You can't believe. If you don't have faith.

Faith is hope and proof for evidence of the unseen. Known only by the wisest.

One doesn't know. What they don't understand.

The wise know. What fools can't dream.

Facts are proven perspectives of differences.

You can't change adversities. At best solve different similarities.

You can't be troubled and grateful at the same time.

One man's enemy. Is another man's hero.

You can't be mad at your enemies. If you never made them angry at you.

You can't hate someone unless you care about them first.

You're never ignorant. If you know the truth.

If you want your enemies to like you. Stay away from them.

If you want fame. Love yourself.

You can only love reality as it is. Not how you want it to be.

Manifestos are stands. We put others on.

A lie can only hurt you. If you believe in it.

You can't make someone like you. That already does.

No one can hurt you. Unless you believe they can.

You can't let go of what. You've never had.

You can't sympathize for pain. If you've never been hurt.

You never have to justify the truth to the wise.

One can't believe in dreams. If they don't.

You can't complain about noise. Without making some.

A lie usually has two sides. The truth has one.

Mother Nature. Is God's will we don't fully understand.

You can't convince someone of the truth. If they're dishonest with themselves.

It's simple to make life more complicated. Than it is.

To understand is half the battle. To win is to know.

The only death in life. Is not to live today.

You haven't lived life to its fullest. Until you've died.

 Insanity is logic denied.

You can't make the insane see. What they don't.

 The light of knowledge. Sets on the darkness of ignorance.

You can't make a wise decision. With the wrong information.

Love has no IQ. The requirement is a wise heart.

Art isn't just technique and talent. It's the courage to create the unknown beauty.

No one can hurt you. If you don't think about it.

If you want someone to forget you. Don't remember them.

My mouth. Is the doorway to my soul.

With love. There's no loser. Only winners.

Injustice has no favorites except itself.

Sanity can sometimes only be a myth. It's a state for the privileged.

There's a fine line between. Persuasion and propaganda.

 Integrity is being accountable for what you've done.

Insanity and genius. Sometimes speak the same language.

 Humility makes no sense. To the arrogant.

You can't play your cards of life and win. Without a full deck.

Fame is useless. To the dead in spirit.

If you know too much. You're stupid.

You don't know what you can't learn. Until you do.

Anger is never a problem. Without thoughts.

You can't be too rich. With nothing.

The man with a thousand ideas. Is no wiser than a dreamer.

It's not that I don't like exercise. It's just that. I don't like moving around.

I don't like what's eating me. More than I like eating.

Coffee is the lubricant of the mind.

I never liked something. I first didn't want.

Reality is always on time. Never late. Always perfect in its ways.

The soul is. The treasure of your being.

You can't walk with God. On your head.

Pain and joy. Baptizes your soul.

To live wisely. Is to be kind to fools and not know it.

Addictions teach a lesson. That ends with disability or death.

Faith is having doubt without proof while hoping for the desired belief of the unseen.

It seems to me it's easier to prove something than disprove it. Can anyone disprove   Jesus's resurrection? Or disprove God's existence? The only answer I have is Faith.

Proof usually has one outcome. Disapproval has infinite possibilities.

There is only one absolute truth. Anything else is fiction.

 Paradoxes are two opposite beliefs which are contradictory.

 If you can believe in the wind, and not see it. Why can't you believe in God or love and not see it?

To prove God's existence. Take a breath. Now where did your first breath come from?
 Hint, not an amoeba.

Religion has been around longer than evolution. Evolution is only a theory that asks questions. Religion answers them.

There is only one God. God has one religion. The one he left behind through him. Our job is to find him with faith. The only reliable truth we have.

There are many roads to the holy summit. Only one path to the top. The rest are dead ends.

Fools don't understand logic. Only stupidity

Tomorrow and yesterday will take care of themselves. If you live in the moment.

You can't change the future. Destiny has already. You can't change the past. Fate has.

Faith is like love. It finds you by surprise.

The wise believe in God's creation. The fool believes in nothing except themselves.

Either you have faith or don't. There's no such thing as an agnostic in God's court.

Who is God? He is the one that was, is, and yet to come. The alpha and the omega. There's only one that fits this description that's written down.

Lies and truth are both written down. To know the difference takes wisdom.

If you have to go to war with others. First go to war with yourself. Then decide the worth of your values.

If you have to correct someone. Correct yourself. Then you might know the difference.

If you don't like someone's behavior. Look at your own.

One can't change someone's mind. Without their permission. In the reality of freedom.

One can't choose between right and wrong. If one doesn't have values.

You can't have freedom. Without different opinions.

You can't change time. Time changes you.

The worst part of pain. Is time.

You can't change a fool from being a fool. If you try it'll be you.

One can change others more. By first changing themselves.

You can learn the most. In the school of life.

You can never be alone. If you love yourself and God.

One doesn't win the race until it's over. It's the same with life.

To put up with others stupidity. You have to use your own genius.

If you want to be on top. You have to start at the bottom.

You can't be mad at others. If you're at peace with yourself.

Life isn't a challenge. If you love it.

The best way to get even with your enemies. Is to pray for justice to take its place.

You can't go to war without first being angry. The trick is to not get angry.

The fastest way out of pain. Is gratitude.

A fools job is to be a fool. That's their role.

Fools hurt others with stupidity. The wise help others with wisdom.

You can't convict the innocent to be guilty without injustice.

One of the best ways out of injustice. Is forgiveness.

Pain can't hurt. If you don't think about it.

The best way to forgive. Is to forget about it.

Words can bring strength and healing. They can also bring pain and sorrow. Words are powerful anywhere.

Greedy people never have enough of. What they don't want.

Just because the villian's caught. Doesn't mean the movie's over.

Whoever hurts God's little children. Hurts God. We are all God's little children. Don't hurt each other.

In the end it's not you who defends or judges yourself on judgement day. It's God.

You can't hurt someone who loves God. And not hurt yourself.

You can't hurt a wise person with insults. Or a fool with praise.

James Peebles Jr.

www.ingramcontent.com/pod-product-compliance
Lightning Source LLC
Chambersburg PA
CBHW031433250726
48656CB00002B/967